BEAUTY, WEALTH, AND POWER

JEWELS AND ORNAMENTS OF ASIA

ASIAN ART MUSEUM OF SAN FRANCISCO

The exhibition *Beauty, Wealth, and Power: Jewels and Ornaments of Asia* has been funded by grants from The Bernard Osher Foundation and the California Arts Council, a state agency. The catalogue has been made possible by a generous contribution from The Society for Asian Art.

Distributed by University of Washington Press, Seattle and London
ISBN 0-295-97201-7

Cover: Necklace (detail). Nepal, late 18th c., gilt silver with semiprecious stones, H. 40 cm (B60 M22+)
Back cover: Netsuke and *inrō* with *inubako* and peach blossoms. Japan, Edo period, late 18th–early 19th c., signed Kajikawa saku, lacquerwork. *Inrō*: H. 8 cm (B70 Y1279); netsuke: H. 2.5 cm (B70 Y1380)
Page one: *A Prince and His Mistress Enjoying Fireworks* (detail). India, Provincial Mughal, 18th c., ink and colors on paper, 55.7 × 34 cm, gift of George Hopper Fitch (B81 D34)

Unless otherwise noted, all reproduced objects are part of The Avery Brundage Collection, Asian Art Museum of San Francisco.

Publication coordinator: So Kam Ng
Photography: Kaz Tsuruta
Editing, design, and production: Marquand Books, Inc.

Printed and bound in Japan

CONTENTS

FOREWORD

Bronze and silver, coral, copper, turquoise, shell, lapis lazuli, feathers, even wood, and, especially in China, jade, in all its magnificent colors, were used for decorating objects to be worn, held, and viewed in the palaces and houses of the powerful throughout Asia. This publication celebrates the prized objects of great civilizations as reflected in the various collections of the Asian Art Museum.

Some of these precious objects were not to be worn during one's lifetime but were specific to burial. The opening of many tombs in Asia has proved the immense wealth of the ancient nobles and their desire to be beautifully adorned throughout eternity.

Among this mass of material one is struck first by the importance of gold, the most malleable and ductile of metals. Retaining its character through the ages, gold came to be an expression of wealth in much of the world and, eventually, a standard for currency. Gold's obvious value has been as splendid decoration, as jewelry and surface ornament. Gold jewelry, while not used as often in early times as that of bronze or silver, was frequently set with colored stones or, especially in eastern Asia, with jade, glass, or semiprecious stones.

One might easily dismiss fabulous jewelry as the leavings of rich or decadent societies, but this would be, I think, a mistake. These luxurious objects demonstrate the high ambitions of brilliant and accomplished people. The art shows, as well, a devotion to craftsmanship and a simple, natural yearning for something that lasts.

Our special appreciation goes to the curators who selected and researched the objects and wrote the informative catalogue essays, sharing their knowledge, enthusiasm, and expertise. Terese Tse Bartholomew and So Kam Ng coordinated the exhibition and catalogue. Hal Fischer facilitated the budget and funding for this project. I also want to extend my appreciation to members of the conservation, registration, and preparator departments as well as other museum support staff who contributed to this effort.

The museum is especially grateful to The Bernard Osher Foundation and its Executive Administrator Patricia Tracy Nagle, the California Arts Council, and The Society for Asian Art for making the exhibition and catalogue possible. We appreciate their support.

Rand Castile
Director

INTRODUCTION

Beauty, Wealth, and Power brings together jewelry and related objects for personal adornment from the major phases of Asia's diverse cultures. This selection is drawn from the permanent collections of the Asian Art Museum of San Francisco and a few generous lenders.

The origins of adorning the human body are lost in the history of early mankind, but the practice must have begun serendipitously when the first prehistoric man or woman attached to the body some fashioned or found object. The first occurrences were, assuredly, profoundly amuletic, as mankind struggled for its existence in a hostile natural world of wild beasts, unpredictable climates, and other unfathomable acts of an alternately violent and beneficent Nature. From this foundation emerged the fashioning of decorative objects for the enhancement of personal appearance, probably first to distinguish important personages such as leaders.

When ritualistic burials first were undertaken, items of personal adornment for the deceased proliferated. Archaeologically retrieved, ancient objects reveal that earrings, hairpins, bracelets, armlets, anklets, finger rings, belts, and toggles were common to both sexes. Later, differentiation of use by sex took place, depending on cultural customs. In addition, burial clothing and wrappings were embedded with elaborate decorative pins or covered with assorted decorative elements of precious metals and pierced stones that were sewn, appliquéd, or draped in garlands onto the textile.

Objects for personal display emerged and developed in Asia according to a variety of amuletic, ritualistic, religious, and secular goals that were conditioned by personal taste, social standing, and the availability of raw materials. Certain forms of personal adornment are expressions of the highest status. The most notable examples have been found in recently discovered hordes of gold-enriched burial suits in Bactria (modern-day Turkestan), elaborate and sumptuous burials in Korea of seventh-century kings and queens resplendent in gold crowns, belts, and jewelry, and the two-thousand-year-old graves of Han royal family members, buried in suits of jade (to achieve, they hoped, immortality) sewn together with threads of gold, silver, or copper, the metal dictated by rank.

The organized religions of Asia revered vast pantheons of icons and other images, and these were often heavily bejeweled. For instance, Sakyamuni, in his earthly life before enlightenment, is depicted as wearing earrings of massive proportions. Representations of him and subsequent Buddha images universally depict his long lobes, a deformation resulting from his wearing of that heavy jewelry. Whether depicted as austerely serene or in vital action, the Hindu gods and goddesses of the South Asian, Himalayan, and Southeast Asian cultural traditions have been bedecked for eternity with rich jewelry. Temple images within holy precincts occasionally are ablaze with jewelry affixed during certain festivals and special regional observances. The ubiquitousness of jewelry has permeated the consciousness of religious practitioners, serving as an impetus for personal emulation and inspiration. Jewelry on icons arose from man's deepest sensitivities about richness and bespeaks a transference of feelings about adornment and identity to a state of reflective consciousness.

Asians have intuitively appreciated the intrinsic beauty and power of certain alloyed materials, ores, and minerals such as gold, silver, bronze, jadeite, nephrite, carnelian, turquoise, coral, diamonds, emeralds, and rubies, along with an assortment of studio-fabricated elements such as glass and enamels. Although all are employed throughout Asia, these precious materials and the form they take through human fabrication are associated more often than not with the distinct features and aspects of the cultures in which they emerge. For instance, the people of Tibet and Mongolia distinguish their jewelry and personal ornaments by a unique, bold handling of metal and semiprecious stones, especially turquoise and coral. Arranged in elaborate patterns, turquoise or coral incrustations are supported by metalwork, heavily or lightly scrolling, depending on the aesthetic mass of the stones. Fabric was also a commonly used ground, especially for headdresses. Worked or natural turquoise nuggets, attractive in their brilliant color, were believed to hold talismanic properties, and the number of stones used reflected status in the social order and sometimes even the locality of creator and wearer.

In contrast to these elaborate compositions are some simple specimens for personal use within Chinese society. In the rich and varied jewelry history of the Chinese, a major genre encompasses belt hooks, belt ornaments, or belt sets made of plaques. Chinese belt accoutrements were made for both the living and the dead, and the vogue for them pulsed sporadically throughout history.

In Japan, jewelry scarcely existed, and rings, necklaces, and earrings had little or no place on the already elaborate traditional Japanese dress. The multiple layering of kimono clothing, each edge revealing and heightening the rhythmic pattern of color, design, and texture, made superfluous any additional embellishment, although lacquer combs and hairpins were often worn by ladies. A unique form of personal adornment did emerge in the later historical eras with the widespread convention among men of wearing a suspended box and toggle (*inrō* and netsuke) at the obi, the traditional sash used to hold the kimono in place.

Thus personal adornment in Asia was a question of culture, history, individual taste, particular beliefs, recurrent courtly extravagance, and geography. The definition of jewelry and finery for personal adornment has been extended within this survey to encompass or distinguish general cultural practices throughout time. The scope of our theme, while limited to representative pieces in the permanent collection, has been made possible by fortunate accidents of survival and archaeological rediscovery or through the careful preservation of heirlooms. Although purchase or donation has allowed some areas and periods to be more richly represented than others, our intent is to highlight available examples of cultural or historical significance.

Clarence F. Shangraw
Chief Curator

LURISTAN

Since the late 1920s a large number of bronzes have appeared on the
world art market from clandestine excavations in central western Iran.
These objects have come to be identified with the mountainous area
of Luristan, a region bordered by present-day Iraq on the west, the
old Baghdad-Hamadan road on the north, the Susiana plain (ancient
Elam) on the south, and the central Iranian plateau on the east.
Because only a fraction of the so-called Luristan bronzes has come
from scientific excavations, a great deal of information has been
irretrievably lost, and many questions about them remain unresolved.

Luristan bronzes of the first millennium B.C. include personal
ornaments as well as military equipment and equestrian gear such as
swords and cheekpieces, suggesting that they were made for warrior-
hunters and their families or a semimobile elite possessing mounted
horsemen and some chariots.[1] These people may have fought with
other tribes or outside populations and lived by hunting game, gather-
ing wild plants and nuts, raising sheep and horses, and practicing some
agriculture. The rather rustic naturalism of the boars' heads (no. 1),
the goat (no. 5), and the pursued caprids (no. 3) reflects a society
keenly observant of animals and close to the wild creatures that were
hunted and that preyed on flocks.

What ties these pastoralists had to particular settlements remains
unclear, but probably the seasonal migration (or transhumance) of
modern tribes represents an ancient way of life. Semiannual move-
ments might have been in response to the unpredictable rainfall, poor
soil, and scarcity of level, tillable land that made total dependence on
farming hazardous.[2] Sheep and goats would have been herded to higher,
cooler pastures in the east in the spring and summer and driven back to
lower, warmer areas in the west in the fall and winter. Valleys of vary-
ing width and slope, intersected by rivers, were natural corridors or
routes along which people moved with their flocks.

The dead often were placed in graves that today seem isolated but
once might have been near campsites. In the Pusht-i Kuh area of south-
western Luristan, for example, cemeteries usually were near a river or
stream and set far enough away to prevent washing out and flooding.
Both men and women were buried with objects of personal adornment
and other grave furnishings. When clear objective evidence has been
lacking, the presence of pins and jewelry has helped to establish the

1. HEAVY TWO-PIECE BRACELET AND BRACELET WITH BOAR-HEAD TERMINALS
Luristan, western Iran, ca. 1000–650 B.C., bronze. Left: W. 8.2 cm (B62 B127); right: W. 6.6 cm (B62 B117)

2. HORSE-SHAPED PIN AND DISC-, ANTELOPE-, AND BIRD-HEADED PINS
Luristan, western Iran, ca. 1000–650 B.C., bronze. Horse (once with iron shank): H. 6 cm, gift of Mr. Ed Nagel (B73 B2); disc: L. 30.5 cm (B62 B80); antelope: L. 18.8 cm (B62 B77); bird: L. 19.3 cm (B62 B56)

graves of women, while the prevalence of tools and weapons has pointed to male burials.[3] There have been difficulties in making clear identifications: both sexes wore earrings, bracelets, and pins, and the difference between a bracelet and anklet, or an anklet and armlet, is not always apparent. Measurements may provide a clue, but a bracelet of small size (as in no. 1, B62 B117) could have been a child's.[4] Men, too, might wear a bracelet as an armlet.

Some archaeologists have postulated that by the late second millennium B.C. iron was still extremely rare, and bronze was the favored material for bracelets and other items.[5] From about 1000 to 750 B.C. a number of bracelets, rings, and pins were made of iron. Iron also was combined with bronze on the same object, as in no. 2, where the horse pinhead is of bronze and the largely missing, corroded shank is of iron. The type of hollow cast bronze bracelet represented in no. 1 (B62 B127) has a counterpart in iron. Bronze, however, was employed for articles of worth and ritual. Indeed, because of the value of the metal, it has been theorized that some bronze objects such as heavy cast "anklets" may have been used as currency or esteemed for their intrinsic metallurgical value.[6]

Moreover, those items thought to be personal ornaments might have had more than strictly secular uses. The heavy weight of the bracelet with bearded heads shown in no. 1 (B62 B127) suggests that it was not worn for "everyday affairs."[7] Pins and pendants might have had apotropaic or religious associations. Pins affixed to the walls of a stone sanctuary at Surkh Dum in eastern Luristan are believed to have had a votive function. Pendants as well as bird- and antelope-headed pins similar to those in no. 2 were also recovered from the shrine.

Straight clothing pins evidently were in use from the third millennium B.C. in western Iran until the fibula (safety pin) became widely fashionable in the seventh century B.C. Although it is known that pins were worn by the living, their exact use in the hair or on clothing remains unclear. Pins have been found at the neck and chest level on or near skeletons, and some have traces of cloth adhering to them. That pins were fastened to clothing with heads facing upward, at an oblique angle, or downward is indicated by representations in art and by the location of pins on or around bodies. Intact suspension chains also suggest that a loop on the shaft (as in no. 4) might once have held an attachment chain to secure the pin to the garment, which might have been of wool or a loosely woven material.

Pinheads were ornamented with both real and fantastic creatures. Despite its "collar" and "tack," the horse in no. 2 looks extraordinary with its forelock, or horn-like projection, and what are often identified as wings. One of the principal themes found on Luristan bronzes is a distinctive version of the "master of animals" motif in which animals flank a central figure. To this category belongs an androgynous, bearded being with breasts and horns, or horned crown, who is confined by two felines (no. 4). These beasts dominate the space with their upright bodies, prominent clawed paws, coiling tails, and monstrous eye rings. Some scholars believe this imagery may reflect local gods, nature demons, or clan deities.

Pendants, which are sometimes mentioned as possibly decorating horse trappings, might have dangled from an individual's belt, as in northwestern Iran, or might have been worn around the wrists, neck, and waist. Pendants in the forms of goats or ibexes (no. 5), birds, dogs, horses, and other creatures might have been associated with deities and worn as amulets. Dogs perhaps had a special protective role in warding off evil spirits or in guarding an owner. Images of certain wild or domestic animals, furthermore, might have been worn to assure success in hunting or the growth and well-being of herds.[8]

Many Luristan bronzes, especially elaborately sculptural ones, were cast by the lost wax process. Details were built up, incised, or tooled in a wax mold, which was then covered with clay and filled with molten metal. Upon cooling, the mold was broken, and the casting finished off. Such objects are thus unique because each piece required a separate mold. On bimetal pins, such as the horse in no. 2, the bronze terminal was cast onto an iron shank. Bronzes were also hammered into sheet metal (as in the disc-headed pin in no. 2) and ornamented with chased or indented relief designs worked from the back side (repoussé). The various trees and oak forests that once covered large areas of Luristan provided fuel for smelting and casting, and beeswax came from local hives in western Iran.

Exactly when and why Luristan bronze production ceased can only be conjectured. It is assumed that as Iranian-speaking peoples gained control of areas and trade routes in western Iran, they undermined the economic and political base of the former Luristan patrons and obstructed their access to metal supplies. Under Cyrus the Great and his successors in the Achaemenid period (550–330 B.C.), Iran was united into an empire that encompassed a vast area from Asia Minor (with its Greek communities) to Afghanistan. The provinces of this far-flung empire were taxed in gold and silver, and gold and silver coins were struck. Lavish jewelry was made, suitable for rulers and their courts, great noble families, and powerful provincial officials.[9]

The opulent use of gold continued in the Hellenistic period after Alexander the Great's conquest in the fourth century B.C. and as the empire broke up into separate regions and dynasties. Greek civilization spread and mingled with local cultures, and jewelry reflected the cosmopolitan influences of diverse craftsmen. The crescent-shaped hoops of no. 6 show the fine workmanship of the Hellenistic period. They are coiled delicately with thin gold wire, fitted with animal heads, and decorated with filigree and engraving. The eyes might have been inlaid

3. PIN WITH PURSUED HORNED ANIMALS
Luristan, western Iran, ca. 1000–650 B.C., bronze, L. 20.9 cm (B62 B132)

5. "GOAT"-SHAPED PENDANT
Luristan, western Iran, ca. 1000–650 B.C.,
bronze, L. 3.5 cm, gift of Mr. Ed Nagel
(B73 B5)

4. PIN WITH OPENWORK HEAD
Luristan, western Iran, ca. 1000–650 B.C.,
bronze, L. 27 cm (B62 B54)

6. TWO EARRINGS (not a pair)
Eastern Mediterranean or Asia Minor, 4th–3rd c. B.C., gold, H. 4.3 and 3.8 cm
(B76 M9a,b)

for a rich polychrome effect. Zoomorphic terminals, long popular in Iran (see no. 1), Assyria, and elsewhere, decorated Achaemenid jewelry and were prominent features on Hellenistic earrings and bracelets. Older concepts and forms not only endured but were revitalized by new allusions and stylistic modifications as they were adapted by craftsmen in various areas.

Diana Turner Fish
Adjunct Associate Curator

NOTES

1. For a discussion of Luristan bronzes, see, for example, P. R. S. Moorey, *Catalogue of the Ancient Persian Bronzes in the Ashmolean Museum* (Oxford: Clarendon Press, 1981), or O. W. Muscarella, *Bronze and Iron: Ancient Near Eastern Artifacts in The Metropolitan Museum of Art* (New York: Metropolitan Museum of Art, 1981), pp. 112ff.

2. E. F. Henrickson, "The Early Development of Pastoralism in the Central Zagros Highlands (Luristan)," *Iranica Antiqua* 20 (1985), pp. 1–42.

3. L. Vanden Berghe, "Les pratiques funéraires à l'âge du Fer 111 au Pusht-i Kuh, Luristan," *Iranica Antiqua* 22 (1987), pp. 223ff.

4. Dr. Guitty Azarpay provided this and other helpful suggestions.

5. Cf., for example, L. Vanden Berghe, "Recherches archéologiques dans le Luristan," *Iranica Antiqua* 10 (1973), pp. 52–55.

6. Moorey, *Ashmolean*, pp. 218, 228; Muscarella, *Bronze and Iron*, pp. 172–73.

7. Muscarella, *Bronze and Iron*, p. 166.

8. For some of these theories, see, for example, E. de Waele, *Bronzes du Luristan et d'Amlash, Ancienne Collection Godard* (Louvain-la-Neuve: Institut Supérieur d'Archéologie et d'Histoire de l'Art, 1982), pp. 181–82; Muscarella, *Bronze and Iron*, pp. 134, 315–16.

9. Gold jewelry is known from a number of pre-Achaemenid sites as well. The writer wishes to thank Dr. David Stronach for his review of the Hellenistic earrings.

INDIA AND THE HIMALAYAS

INDIA

The jewelry and ornaments of the many regions of India are sumptuously
varied and complex. Much of what we know about this rich tradition
comes from sculptural depictions. From the terra-cotta images and the
stone sculptures of the Shunga period (second to first century B.C.),
we know that in prehistoric times Indian women and men ornamented
their bodies with strands of pearls and beads. Earrings—so heavy that
they distended earlobes—took on elaborate shapes: circles, squares,
clusters, pendants, and animals, both real and imaginary. Arm clasps
and bracelets were common, as were heavy anklets, finger rings, and
toe rings. Men and women wore elaborate hairdos, wound with strands
of beads and other ornaments. The broad hips of the slender-waisted
yakshi, female fertility spirits, were adorned with wide bands of ornaments. Besides serving the basic human desire for adornment, the
luxurious jewelry portrayed wealth and status in ancient India.

Ancient India.
      The sculpture of Gandhara (modern-day southern Afghanistan
and northern Pakistan) presents a very different style of jewelry. Part of
the Kushan empire, Gandhara was situated on the crossroads between
east and west, and its Buddhist art shows a wonderful fusion of Graeco-
Roman, Scythian, and Central Asian styles, but with Indian iconogra-
phy. When images of Buddha appeared around the second century
A.D., he was shown with distended earlobes, deformed by the heavy
earrings he wore as a prince. While Buddha wears the simple garments
of a monk, images of the bodhisattva are arrayed in princely attire,
elaborately coiffed and bejeweled. A Kushan Bodhisattva Maitreya
(no. 1) wears a crescent moon, flowers, and strands of pearls in his
hair. Lion earrings ornament his ears, and a heavy necklace set with
roughly faceted stones adorns his neck. A main necklace of twisted
pearl strands supports a pendant of two centaurs carrying an amulet
box. Three thinner necklaces, strung with small amulet boxes, cross
his chest and upper right arm. Tied on his upper arms are trefoil-
shaped ornaments, again set with faceted stones.

Gandharan jewelry, mainly earrings and small gold ornaments,
has been excavated from archaeological sites and found inside stone
reliquaries. The earrings shown in no. 2 are elegant creations in gold

1. BODHISATTVA MAITREYA
Gandhara, India, Kushan period, 2nd–3rd c., phyllite, H. 115 cm (B60 S597)

2. PAIR OF EARRINGS
Gandhara, India, 4th–5th c., gold and garnets, D. 2 cm, gift of the M. J. Engel Memorial Fund
(B86 M6a,b)

3. SEATED GANESHA
Mysore, India, Hoysala period, 13th c., chloritic schist, H. 90.2 cm,
gift of the de Young Museum Society (B68 S4)

and garnet. Typical of Gandharan earrings, they combine globules and
fine granulation, displaying an affinity with Scythian jewelry.

A thirteenth-century elephant-headed Ganesha from Mysore
(no. 3) epitomizes India's medieval jewelry tradition. Like the icing
on a European wedding cake, the headdress of the Lord of Obstacles
is a masterful creation of descending bands encrusted with jewels,
suspended with loops and tassels of pearl-like gems. Besides the usual
bracelets, arm clasps, and anklets, Ganesha wears ear cuffs and finger
and toe rings. *Kirttimukha* (face of glory) masks embellish his tusks,
and numerous necklaces cascade from his neck and shoulders, across
his chest, and around his torso.

When the Mughals came to power in the sixteenth century, they
brought with them the jade and jewels favored by their Timurid ancestors and the Persian court. Manuscript paintings show emperors and
princes attired in silks and brocades, wearing gems and strands of
pearls, and sporting weapons with elaborately ornamented hilts,
sheaths, and chapes (see page 1). Precious gems were believed to bring
health and protection: the emerald was good for one's sight, the pearl
dissolved blood clots in the heart and stopped hemorrhages, and the

diamond brought good fortune.[1] Gems such as emeralds and spinels were roughly polished or tumbled. They were also made into cabochons or carved with designs. The choker of no. 4 shows a combination of tumbled emeralds with pearls and diamonds in gold openwork. Gold and gems were often combined with enamels, a technique that came from the West.

The Mughals especially favored jade, and their jade carving skill was well known throughout Asia. The Qianlong emperor of China held Mughal jade in such high esteem that he composed poetry in praise of it, and he ordered his palace workshop to imitate India's thin-walled jade vessels decorated with luxuriant floral motifs. Associated with victory, jade was fashioned into the hilts of knives and daggers to bring success to their owners. Jade was also purported to cure stomach ailments and was worn around the neck for its restorative benefit.

Gold, because of its color, is considered a "solar" metal in India. Besides being the favorite metal for personal adornment, pure gold is also preferred for sacrificial purposes. Jewelry made of gold and silver is known as "Ganga-Jamuna"; the gold symbolizes the golden waters of the sacred Ganges River, while silver represents the silvery waters of its tributary, the Jamuna.

Indian gold jewelry of the nineteenth and twentieth centuries represents a tradition that goes back thousands of years. Gold jewelry is one of the main components of a woman's dowry, and according to Hindu law, followed by Jains and Sikhs as well, a dowry belongs to a woman for life, to be disposed of as she pleases. Gold jewelry is more than an Indian woman's personal adornment; it is her entitlement and a provision against unfortunate circumstances.

NEPAL

A set of jewelry from Nepal (no. 5) epitomizes the creativity and superb craftsmanship of the Newar people of the Kathmandu Valley. A tour de force of inlay and filigree work, the group consists of a pendant, earrings, a reliquary box, and a belt buckle. Each piece is lavishly set with gems and semiprecious materials: turquoise, coral, rubies, tourmalines, mother-of-pearl, and conch shell. In the pendant a center piece of carved turquoise depicts the multiarmed goddess Durga vanquishing the buffalo demon, flanked by two carved images of tantric deities with numerous arms. On the earrings are images of the god Vishnu riding on the sun-bird Garuda, who steps on a pair of snake deities. The same motif is repeated on the reliquary, where the group flies above the snowy peaks of Nepal. Ornamenting the ends of the belt buckle are *kirttimukha* masks. This protective motif originated in India but is widely used in Nepal.

4. JEWELED CHOKER
India, 19th c., gold, pearls, diamonds, and emeralds, L. 25 cm (B76 M47)

5. SET OF JEWELRY (necklace, *gau*, earrings, and belt buckle)
Nepal, late 18th c., gilt silver with semiprecious stones, H. (earrings) 7.5 cm (B60 M22–26+)

TIBET

Around 1929 the thirteenth Dalai Lama decreed that women were not to keep or wear an abundance of precious and expensive ornaments, for he observed that fascination with them was driving many families into debt and hardship. He further stated that "women from families of the fourth rank or above should wear only the *mutig patruk* [pearl head-dress] and jewelry worth no more than five hundred *dotse*, while the lower class women should wear only a plain *patruk* and should not wear jewelry exceeding two hundred fifty *dotse* in worth."[2] Considering that six *dotse* could purchase an ounce of gold in those days, the stern mandate did not seem too harsh. For a few years the women of Lhasa tried to comply with the decree, but the craze for elaborate jewelry revived soon after the Dalai Lama's death in 1933. An affluent lady in Lhasa and central Tibet around the early twentieth century would have possessed sixteen different types of jewelry made from gold and silver and set with semiprecious and precious stones such as turquoise, pearls, jade, and even diamonds.[3] The pieces would have included a headdress, necklaces, *gau* (reliquary box), earrings, ear ornaments, strings of pearls for the hair, a purse, needle case, and various pendants. As many as twelve kinds of jewelry would be worn on formal occasions.

Tibetan jewelry differs from region to region and varies with rank and status. According to an account published in the early 1950s, "Every man was obliged to present his wife with the jewels corresponding to his rank. Promotion in rank entailed promotion in jewelry! But to be merely rich was not enough, for wealth did not confer the right to wear costly jewels."[4]

The *patruk* mentioned by the Dalai Lama is the headdress of the Lhasa area. Its Y-shaped form is made of rolled cotton tubes covered with red wool and embellished with turquoise, coral, and pearl. The *mutig patruk*, or pearl headdress, has "fourteen red corals the size of a large hen's egg and eight turquoises the size of marbles, as well as many seed pearls."[5] Ladies from the Tsang area wore a bow-shaped headdress, extending about a foot from each side of the head, that was strung with pearls and decorated with turquoise and coral. Jamyang Sakya described how it felt to wear a Tsang headdress shortly after her marriage into the royal family of Sakya: "The headdress weighed about twenty-five pounds and severely limited one's movement. In just a short while, balancing this headpiece brought a stiff neck."[6]

A typical *perak* from Ladakh (no. 6), another kind of headdress, showing an impressive array of turquoise, consists of a padded triangular piece of red cloth in front that tapers to a square end. Earflaps of black sheep's wool starkly contrast the rows of variously colored turquoise running the length of the headdress. A *gau*, of blue glass and pieces of carnelian, and a silver ornament with tassels adorn the triangular section. A side panel displays strands of coral, while tassels

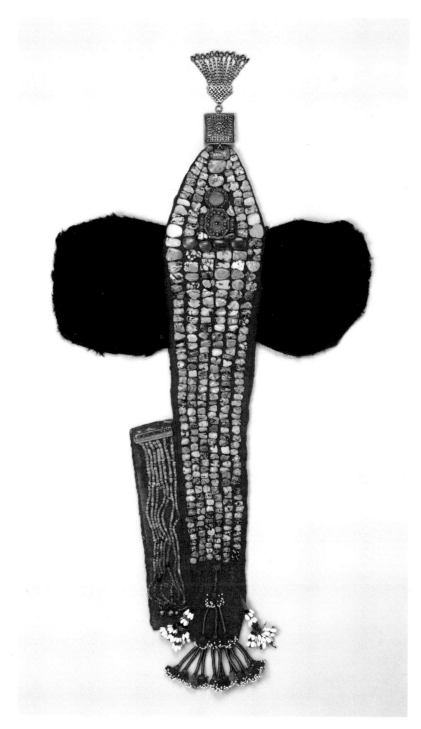

6. PERAK
Ladakh, India, 20th c., turquoise, coral, carnelian, shells, silver, glass, lambskin, and cotton, L. 99 cm, gift of Raymond G. and Milla L. Handley (1991.94)

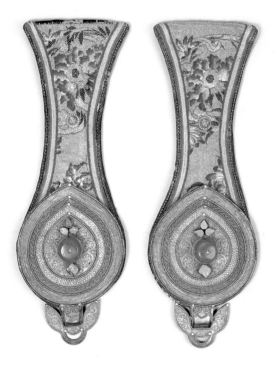

7. PAIR OF CHATELAINES
Amdo, Tibet, early 20th c., silver, turquoise, coral, and Russian brocade, L. 33.3 cm, gift of Paul and Jacquelyn Ronan (1990.192.1–.2)

8. RELIQUARY BOXES (*gau*)
Tibet, 18th–19th c., silver and copper with inlaid stones. Oval: w. 11.4 cm (B60 M449); rectangular: w. 6.7 cm (B60 M452); shrine-shaped: w. 8.9 cm (B60 M453)

of white shells and beads decorate the square end. Turquoise (Tibetan: *yu*) is a favorite stone in Tibet, and although some is found there, a large amount comes from China, Afghanistan, and elsewhere. The bright blue ones in the *perak* are from the People's Republic of China.

In Kham, or eastern Tibet, married women wear turquoise, coral, amber, and *gzi* beads in their braided hair. The silversmiths of Derge in eastern Tibet are noted for their filigree work, and a pair of chatelaines (no. 7) is representative of their skill. A large silver ornament, partially gilded, is filled with concentric bands of beading, braiding, and fine filigree work and set with coral and turquoise. A small gilded piece at the bottom has an opening through which one can attach keys, eating sets of knives and chopsticks, or other useful items. The ornament is connected to a loop made of Russian brocade and edged with leather and chain stitches. Many eastern Tibetans are nomads, and they often suspend such ingeniously designed devices from their belts to free their hands for other work.

The *gau* is one of the most important personal adornments of Tibet (no. 8). This beautiful ornament, a receptacle for small images, printed prayers and charms, *tsha tsha* (small clay votive plaques), and other relics, is worn traditionally by both men and women to ward off evil. The top of the *gau*, usually of silver, has fine filigree work and can be embellished with turquoise and coral; the plain back is removable so that relics can be inserted. Elaborate examples worn by the elite are made of gold and turquoise. While women wear their *gau* on a short necklace around their necks, strung with turquoise, coral, or *gzi* beads (no. 9), a man's *gau* is larger and often shaped like a shrine. A traveler straps the *gau* to the arm or wears it across the chest, bandolier style (no. 10). The traveling *gau* is sometimes encased in brocade and placed on the family altar when not in use.

On formal occasions such as the New Year celebration, Tibetan officials wore the *gya-lu che* costume ("the garment of royalty," a complex assemblage representing the costume of the ancient Tibetan). Part of the costume's regalia is a pair of turquoise and gold ornaments, one shaped like a whelk shell and the other a flat rosette, strung together and worn across one's shoulders. The ceremonial ornament of no. 11 was once part of this regalia (the rosette is missing). This unique object has seven decorative bands separated by gold beading and inlaid with turquoise. A *khyung* bird (Sanskrit: Garuda) of turquoise, ruby, and lapis lazuli surmounts the top. Originally from India, the *khyung* motif occurs often in Himalayan art and acts as an apotropaic agent.

Two ornaments most highly valued by Tibetans are *gzi* beads and *thog-lchags*. A *gzi* is a barrel-shaped agate bead with markings of stripes and circles (no. 12). It can be a naturally banded agate or an agate etched or stained by means of an ancient technique not fully understood at this time. Tibetans believe that *gzi* beads are found objects of

9. Tibetan woman wearing a *gau* and *gzi* beads. Photo by Michael Levin.

10. Tibetan man wearing a *gau*. Photo by Michael Levin.

11. CEREMONIAL ORNAMENT
Tibet, 19th c., gold, turquoise, and lapis lazuli,
L. 9.5 cm, gift of Margaret Polak (B87 M18)

12. GZI BEADS
Tibet, date unknown, agate, w. 1.6–12 cm
(anonymous loans)

supernatural origin holding great magical power; some feel that *gzi* were worms crawling in the earth before they were killed by a human touch. Gzi beads, many of which come from eastern Tibet, command fabulous prices, especially those with odd numbers of eyes. They are worn singly around the neck or in combination with other beads for protection against demons who can cause sudden death. Tibetans are very reluctant to sell their *gzi* beads, believing that misfortune will soon follow if they do.

Thog-lchags (no. 13) are small metal ornaments unearthed by peasants in the fields or picked up by nomads in the highlands. Like *gzi* beads, they are believed to be powerful talismans that ward off evil, and Tibetans are loath to part with them, especially if they are lucky enough to find nine examples, nine being a sacred number in pre-Buddhist beliefs.

Thog-lchags come in a variety of shapes, sizes, and motifs. They include the gods of Tibet, religious objects such as tiny *dorje* (thunderbolt) and *phurbu* (triangular peg-like dagger), plaques with mantras, *khyung* birds and animals, arrowheads, remnants of horse trappings, clasps, bells, and rattles. Although some are found in Tibet or locally manufactured, *thog-lchags* can be Chinese, Nepalese, Indian, and even Scythian in origin, brought into the region by the various travelers who once traversed the Tibetan plateau. Some arrowheads and pieces of horse trappings are actually Ordos bronzes originating in Inner Mongolia and dating to the Han dynasty.

13. *THOG-LCHAGS*
Tibet, Nepal, Inner Mongolia, and China, dates unknown, bronze,
H. 4–8.2 cm (anonymous loans)

BHUTAN

The kingdom of Bhutan lies in the eastern Himalayas, between Tibet and India. As in Tibet, Buddhism permeates the life of the population and is especially reflected in their arts. The Bhutanese are well known for their silver ornaments such as the pair of silver pins depicted in no. 14. Such pins were used earlier in this century to secure a woman's garment, the *kira*, at the shoulders. The ring at the top is decorated with *makara* heads (a crocodile-like mythical beast) and finely engraved designs. The pin, ornamented with turquoise, has a spiralling shaft, elegantly engraved in the middle section, and tapers to a sharp point. Nowadays women wear silver *komas* instead—medallions (usually in the shape of Buddhist symbols) with sharp hooks in the back, linked by a chain. Men of means carry silver betel boxes and lime boxes inside their garments and fancy swords with silver hilts and scabbards in openwork, gilded and embellished with turquoise. Like their Tibetan neighbors, Bhutanese women also wear necklaces of turquoise, coral, and *gzi* beads.

14. PAIR OF SILVER PINS
Bhutan, early 20th c., silver and turquoise,
L. 19.7 cm, gift of Tashi Dorji (1990.237)

15. HEADDRESS
Ordos, Mongolia, early 20th c., padded
cotton with coral and turquoise beads, with
silver ornaments encrusted with semiprecious
stones, L. 48.7 cm, gift of Ursula Wolcott
Griswold Bingham (B87 M15.5)

MONGOLIA

Mongolian women are famous for their fantastic headdresses. Even
in the Yuan dynasty (1260–1368), official portraits show Mongol
empresses wearing towering headdresses and ear ornaments of jewels
and pearls. Hair ornaments differ from tribe to tribe, each vying with
the other for greater splendor.

The Ordos Mongols, according to tradition, are the descendants of
Genghis Khan's bodyguard. This tribe lives in Inner Mongolia, north
of the Great Wall, bordered by the Yellow River on three sides. When
compared to the headdresses of other Mongol tribes, the Ordos example (no. 15) is a simple yet elegant creation, consisting of a wide
padded fillet, two earflaps, and a neck flap in indigo cotton with two
side hangings, completely covered with silver plaques and coral and
turquoise beads. An elaborate network of silver beads forms a fringe
for the forehead. The headdress is accompanied by a necklace and
exquisite ear ornaments complete with small silver amulet boxes and
tassels of silver and turquoise beads.

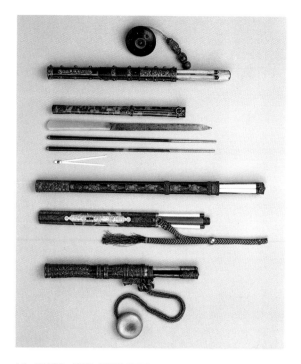

16. KNIFE AND CHOPSTICKS SETS
Mongolia and China, 19th and 20th c., metal, wood, ivory, and silver with coral malachite, turquoise, carnelian, glass, and agate, L. 7.5–25.4 cm. Top to bottom: gift of Ursula Wolcott Griswold Bingham (B87 M15.3), The Avery Brundage Collection (B76 M12, B65 M12), gift of Captain and Mrs. Barrett G. Hindes (B81 M43), gift of Ursula Wolcott Griswold Bingham (B87 M15.2)

Mongolians, like the nomadic Tibetans and Manchurians, also attach flint and tinder pouches and eating sets to their sashes. The Asian version of a Swiss army knife, the eating set is ingeniously designed to carry a sharp knife and a pair of chopsticks, and sometimes a toothpick and an ear scratcher (no. 16). Some of the fancier containers are elaborately inlaid with tortoiseshell and embellished with malachite and coral.

Terese Tse Bartholomew
Curator of Indian and Himalayan Art

NOTES

1. Michael Spink, "Some Aspects of Islamic Jewellery," in *Islamic and Hindu Jewellery* (London: Spink and Son Ltd., 1988), pp. 9–11.

2. Dorje Yudon Yutok, *House of the Turquoise Roof* (New York: Snow Lion Publications, 1990), p. 189.

3. Ibid., p. 185.

4. Heinrich Harrer, *Seven Years in Tibet* (New York: E. P. Dutton & Co., 1953), p. 142.

5. Yutok, *House of the Turquoise Roof*, p. 321.

6. Jamyang Sakya and Julie Emery, *Princess in the Land of Snows* (Boston: Shambala Publications, 1990), p. 102.

SOUTHEAST ASIA

PREHISTORIC PERIOD IN SOUTHEAST ASIA

The earliest known adornment in Southeast Asia is jewelry from the third millennium B.C. Shell and stone jewelry from various cultures of this prehistoric period displays a surprising homogeneity, consistent with the assumption that cultural ties linked the mainland and insular Southeast Asia. Excavated at burial sites, these pieces suggest a belief in the afterlife or a reverence for ancestors.

The earliest Southeast Asian ornaments in the Asian Art Museum collection were excavated from burial sites at Ban Chiang, in northeastern Thailand. In 1966 Stephen Young, son of the American ambassador to Thailand, recognized the importance of a group of large painted jars that had been discovered in the village. Subsequent excavations carried out by the Fine Arts Department (and illegal looting by local villagers) uncovered many burials replete with pots, bronze implements, and bronze, stone, and glass jewelry.

The bronze jewelry, which has been dated to the end of the Ban Chiang culture (800 B.C.–A.D. 500), exhibits a variety of forms and decorative motifs (no. 1). A bracelet with bells jingles when shaken (B80 B4); a spiraled circle, the only motif on a simple bracelet (B80 B3), is combined with striations on a wider one (1989.7.12). Bracelets varied radically in size; some, judging by their small diameters, were obviously worn by children.

The ability to mine and work gold effected a change in the material culture of all Southeast Asia. The precious metal, an impermeable and valued offering to ancestors, was abundant throughout the region. Indonesian and Philippine burials from the first millennium A.D. included thin gold sheets to cover the eyes, nose, and mouth of the deceased. A scientifically excavated Balinese site gives an early date of A.D. 100 to these masks.[1]

Early Indian texts, such as the *Rāmāyana* and the Buddhist *jātaka* tales, mention Suvarnabhūmi, land of gold, and Suvarnadvīpa, island of gold;[2] Ptolomy also made reference to Southeast Asian gold. These legends of wealth attracted Arab and Western traders. The first-century edict of the Roman emperor Vespasian had prohibited the export of gold from the empire, necessitating a new source. The development of more seaworthy ships in the early centuries of the first millennium A.D., the longing for the luxury goods of China, and the

1. BRONZE BRACELETS
Thailand, Ban Chiang culture, 800 B.C.–A.D. 500. Left: H. 14.6 cm, gift of Mr. and Mrs. Frank
H. Koehler (1989.7.12); upper right: D. 8.8 cm, gift of Joy French Black (B80 B3); lower right:
W. 9 cm, gift of Joy French Black (B80 B4)

exhausted state of South Indian mines by the third century A.D. gave
additional impetus to these early traders.

Another significant event of the early centuries of the first millennium A.D. in Southeast Asia was the arrival of Indian Buddhist and
Hindu thought, culture, and art styles. We know little of this period
because only in the fifth century did inscriptional evidence and archaeological remains begin to clarify local history, but by the seventh to
eighth centuries the full impact of the two great Indian religions was
felt both on the mainland and in the islands.

By this time the coastal regions of Southeast Asia were participat-
ing in extensive trade with China and the West. Gold and jewels are
mentioned repeatedly in early sources. A seventh-century Chinese
history describing the Malay Peninsula noted:

> The king and his high officials add cloths of *yun-hsia* to cover their
> shoulders, wear golden cords as girdles, and insert gold rings in
> their ears. The women wrap themselves in cotton cloths and coil
> jewelled cinctures about their bodies.[3]

MYANMAR (BURMA)

In the Pyu kingdom in Myanmar (formerly Burma) and the Mon-
Dvaravati kingdom that extended from Myanmar through southern and

2. INTAGLIOS
Myanmar, Pyu period, 7th–10th c. Left to right: carnelian, w. 2.7 cm, gift in honor of Leath
and Heather Castile (1989.5.2); agate, w. 1.2 cm, gift in honor of Leath and Heather Castile
(1989.46.2); agate, w. 2.4 cm, gift of Mrs. Virginia Lee Taylor (1989.14.2)

central Thailand, jewelry was buried in the foundations of Buddhist
stupas and temples.

The Pyu intaglios included here, like contemporary intaglios found
in southern Vietnam and Cambodia, indicate a knowledge of Western
jewelry making (no. 2). However, unlike Greek and Roman intaglios,
which include representations of specific myths, the Pyu motifs consist
of single animals, generally unidentifiable. An unusual example is
decorated with a bull with a moon above his back (1989.5.2). The bull
Nandi is Śiva's mount, and the moon often symbolizes Śiva, thus suggesting an association with this Hindu god. Intaglios have been found
throughout Southeast Asia, often set in rings, yet the largest numbers
of intaglios are from the mainland and were probably produced there.

While gold, intaglios, and beads form the bulk of early Myanmari
jewelry, later jewelers (from the twelfth century) made use of the abundant gemstones for which the country is renowned. The stones were set
in resin in gold rings, pendants, and earrings. Beads included not only
simple glass and stone but tiny fanciful animals—elephants, turtles,
and birds.

INDONESIA
In the nineteenth century, the Batavia Museum, now the Nasional
Museum, Jakarta, Java, stopped accepting Hindu-Buddhist period
(seventh–sixteenth century) gold jewelry. Such large quantities of gold

rings, ear ornaments, cords, bracelets, belt buckles, and glass beads had been brought to them that they felt they owned enough!

Early accounts, in the form of poems and inscriptions dedicating temples and temple land, describe not only jewelry but its ritual uses. As in Myanmar and Thailand, gold was considered a worthy material for burial in the foundation of a temple. Gold rings called *prasada voh:* were given to participants in the dedication of a temple. The rings were of prescribed weights that were in accord with the importance of the person receiving the gift.[4]

Stone and bronze Javanese sculpture offers visual evidence of jewelry styles and the often excessive (by modern Western standards) use of ornament. Ropes of gold hang from the necks and waists of these figures. Armbands, often gold repoussé attached to cloth bands, and bracelets extend from wrist to upper arm, while rings adorn all finger joints. Ear ornaments not only hang from pierced holes but function as cuffs along the distended lobes. While the common man certainly was less richly adorned, early Western travelers marveled at the abundance of jewelry worn by the islanders; the effect was dazzling.

Ear ornaments were cast and forged in a range of styles (no. 3). A pair of cuffs (1988.15a, b) illustrates the apparently popular geometric style, a series of circles and squares that ends with a flame-like flourish. The cuffs were probably attached to the upper part of the distended lobe. A heavier, single ear cuff (87 M17), decorated with the popular eastern Javanese cloud motif, is an appropriate contrast to the regularized pattern of the geometric pair.[5]

The fantastic *makara* with an elephant's trunk was a standard architectural element on Indonesian Hindu and Buddhist temples. As marvelous as the motif looks on this ear ornament (1988.19), it is difficult to imagine how the ornament would have balanced on the distended lobe. Another ear cuff (1990.203) is so small that it may have been used as a ring for a pigeon's leg. This example is set with rubies, with the lower one set in place with resin. The angularity of some ear ornaments differs radically from the softer, more fluid style of earlier jewelry, thus representing a late Hindu-Buddhist style.

The heavy cast or forged rings that have been found in Java in such abundance might be *prasada voh:*, rings known to have been given to increase a temple donor's status but not clearly described in ancient texts. The more delicate ring included in no. 3 (1988.14) is adorned with the so-called Śrī motif found on many heavier rings. This Sanskrit honorific or symbol of the goddess Śrī was displayed in endless permutations on mainland and insular Southeast Asian rings of the seventh through tenth century.[6]

Glass beads (no. 4) were produced in Southeast Asia and have been found in prehistoric burial sites as well as in household treasures. Millefiori beads were valued in their many sizes, colors, shapes, and

3. GOLD EAR ORNAMENTS AND RING

Java, Indonesia, 9th–14th c., H. 1.5–1.8 cm. Top, left to right: gift of Mrs. Linda Noe Laine in memory of the Honorable Clare Booth Luce (87 M17); gift of Marjorie Bissinger Seller (1988.19); gift of Marjorie Bissinger Seller and Marion Greene (1988.15a–b). Bottom, left to right: gift of Mrs. Virginia Lee Taylor (1988.14); purchased by Asian Art Museum General Acquisition Fund (1991.229, 1990.203)

4. GLASS BEAD NECKLACE AND MILLEFIORI BEADS

Java, Indonesia, Majapahit period, 14th–15th c. Necklace: L. 109.2 cm, beads (avg.): W. 2.4 cm, gift of Mrs. Brayton Wilbur, Jr. (1988.64.1, 1988.64.2a–d)

5. GOLD BRACELETS
Philippines, c. 1200, D. 6.8 cm, promised gift of Mrs. Yolanda Ortega-Stern (R1991.13.1–.6)

decorative surfaces. Gravediggers have found them placed over the eyes, nose, ears, mouth, navel, and genitals of eastern Javanese corpses.[7] Only in recent centuries have Western trade beads become common in Asia.[8]

PHILIPPINES
The Philippines, today the sixth largest producer of gold in the world, was an important source in the prehispanic period (prior to the six-teenth century). Unlike the literary, inscriptional, and sculptural sources that help contextualize Indonesian adornment, Philippine his-tory and culture prior to the sixteenth century is known from a few archaeological excavations and foreign accounts of the islands. One seventeenth-century Spanish author wrote:

> Their whole adornment consists in having very rich and beautiful necklaces, earrings and gold rings or bracelets. They wear those bracelets above the ankle; some wear these of ivory, and others of brass. They also have little round plates three fingers in diameter, which they pass through a hole that they make in the ear.[9]

As in other Southeast Asian countries, stone, glass, and shell were used for prehistoric jewelry, with gold becoming popular in the first millennium A.D. Like Indonesian jewelry, the abundant Philippine gold artifacts have been recovered by chance. Gold chains, bracelets, rings, and ear ornaments are the most commonly encountered adorn-ments, but only crucibles, goldworking tools, and a few gold pieces

6. Illustration of a Visayan couple from the Boxer Codex. Late 16th c., collection of Dr. C. R. Boxer.

have been uncovered in scientific excavations. Because of this lack of context, our ability to date gold Filipino jewelry is limited.

Gold of the prehispanic period was generally forged or worked in repoussé. Heavy gold rings with the Śri motif and Garuda pendants hint at Hindu and Buddhist inroads into a culture that appears to have remained relatively aloof from outside influence until the coming of the Spanish. Styles and types of other jewelry suggest trade links throughout Asia; for example, some repoussé bracelets found in the Philippines (no. 5) are similar to those discovered on Sulawesi.[10] The large number found in the Philippines, however, compared to a smaller quantity from Indonesia, implies they were of Philippine origin.

7. *MAMULI*
Java, Indonesia, 19th–20th c., gold, w. 5 cm, gift of Mrs. Brayton Wilbur, Jr. (1988.64.4)

The Boxer Codex, a sixteenth-century Spanish text with descriptive accounts of Asian lands and peoples, records the dress and jewelry of the Filipinos (no. 6). If the paintings in the Boxer Codex give us a true indication of the jewelry worn at the time of the Spanish conquest, we can surmise that the bracelet was the most common ornament. Most of the men and women depicted wear multiple bracelets on both arms. The most common gold bracelets are a plain narrow band and a narrow band with repoussé work. The repoussé designs alternate small and large dots of differing shapes, and when the bracelets were worn together, the variations would have created interesting textures.

The traditions of personal adornment begun in the prehistoric period and altered throughout the second millennium A.D. continue today in insular and mainland Southeast Asia. In northeastern Thailand, Laos, Myanmar, and Vietnam, tribal women wear bracelets of silver that jingle as the Ban Chiang bracelets did. In insular Southeast Asia, repoussé goldwork has been Islamized, and in the Philippines westernized, yet jewelers continue to produce exquisite jewelry. Traditional materials are now used in innovative ways. Beads are still included in household treasures throughout the region, both as necklaces and as part of intricate work on clothing, baby carriers, and hats. Shell is combined with hornbill beak in elegant earrings by the Ilongot peoples of the Philippines.

Yet one fantastic headdress, the *marannga* from West Sumba, is unrelated to any ancient jewelry we know. It and the gilt silver bracelets of the Batak in Sumatra provide only a hint of the diversity of nineteenth- and twentieth-century works.

The *mamuli* from Sumba (no. 7) derives from an ancient shape known throughout insular Southeast Asia. We do not know what the earlier form, worn both as an ear ornament and as a pendant, symbolized in ancient times. But today the *mamuli* forms a part of the bridewealth in the complex ritual of gift exchange in Sumba. More elaborate versions find a place on the house altar as a portion of the household treasure.

Nancy Hock
Paul L. and Phyllis Wattis Foundation Curator of Southeast Asian Art

NOTES

1. R. P. Soejono, "The Significance of the Excavations at Gilimanuk (Bali)," in *Early Southeast Asia*, ed. R. B. Smith and W. Watson (New York: Oxford University Press, 1979), pp. 185–98; and "Sistim-sistim penguburan pada Akhir Masa Prasejarah di Bali," Ph.D. diss., Universitas Indonesia, 1977, referred to in John N. Miksic, *Old Javanese Gold* (Singapore: Ideation, 1989), p. 40.

2. See Paul Wheatley, *The Golden Khersonese* (1961; reprint, Westport, Conn.: Greenwood Press, 1973), pp. 177–84, for a discussion of Indian sources that make reference to these and associated names.

3. *Liang-shu*, chap. 54, fol. 18 recto et seq., as quoted in Wheatley, *The Golden Khersonese*, pp. 253–54.

4. For examples of gold given in tribute, see Himansu Bhusan Sarkar, *Corpus of the Inscriptions of Java* (Calcutta: Firma K. L. Mukhopadhyay, 1971), I:71, 283–84; II:2, 17, 31. See I:24 for gifts to participants.

5. The mate to this ear ornament is in a New York collection.

6. F. D. K. Bosch, "Gouden vingerringen uit de Hindoe-Javaansche tigdperk," *Djawa* 7 (1927), pp. 305–20.

7. R. K. Liu, "Indonesian Glass Beads," *Ornament* 9, no. 4 (Summer 1986), p. 65.

8. Peter Francis, Jr., "Glass Beads in Asia," *Asian Perspectives* 28, no. 1 (1988–89), p. 16.

9. Emmett Blair and James A. Robertson, eds., *The Philippine Islands 1493–1898*, vol. 29, "Relation of the Filipinas Islands" [S. J. Diego de Bobadilla, 1640] (Cleveland: Arthur H. Clark Co., 1903–9), p. 286.

10. See comparable examples from Sulawesi in the Birmingham Museum of Art, Alabama.

CHINA

In China jewelry has been used to heighten personal allure since the beginning of human history. Both men and women wore it for its appeal to the eyes as well as the ears, to enliven points of beauty (especially ears, hair, wrist, and waist), and to create an ambiance of elegant sensuality. But within the tightly organized social scheme of Confucianism, jewelry was also designed to arouse a sense of civilized propriety. In the Zhou dynasty (eleventh–third century B.C.) restrained jewels signaled a man or woman of culture and reinforced rank; they were tokens of friendship and trust—a continuing theme in early Chinese poetry—and, in later dynasties, marks of ethnic identity.

For the Chinese, jewelry was so much a necessary component of civilization that neglecting it, rejecting it, or misusing it could be seen as a dangerous renunciation of social norms. The complicated regulations governing every aspect of Confucian society affected not only the living but also the dead. Reinstated in an alternate but material universe, the dead were adorned with jewelry for many of the same reasons as the living: to reinforce rank, to symbolize bonds of trust, and even to beautify the body. But the precious gems worn by the dead had added meaning; some, especially jade and gold, were believed to prevent corruption of the flesh and guarantee physical immortality, a goal that by the Han dynasty (206 B.C.–A.D. 220) was nearly all consuming.

JEWELRY FOR THE DEAD

Even in earliest prehistory, mortuary jewelry may have served a protective function, averting evil and preserving the body's integrity. At Zhougoudian, near Beijing, in a palaeolithic stratum dating to ten or twenty thousand years ago, skeletal remains have been found surrounded with perforated teeth, shells, and fish bones. By neolithic times, especially in the Liangzhu culture centered around present-day Shanghai (ca. 3500–2000 B.C.), elite burials were packed with jade *bi* discs and *cong* tubes (much later, in the Han dynasty, symbols of heaven and earth) and jade plaques and laminae incised with monstrous faces, sometimes numbering in the hundreds. In the northern neolithic culture of Hongshan (ca. 3500–2000 B.C.) in Inner Mongolia, some select dead had flaring tubes of jade placed at the napes of their necks, as either hair clasps or neck rests (no. 1); others

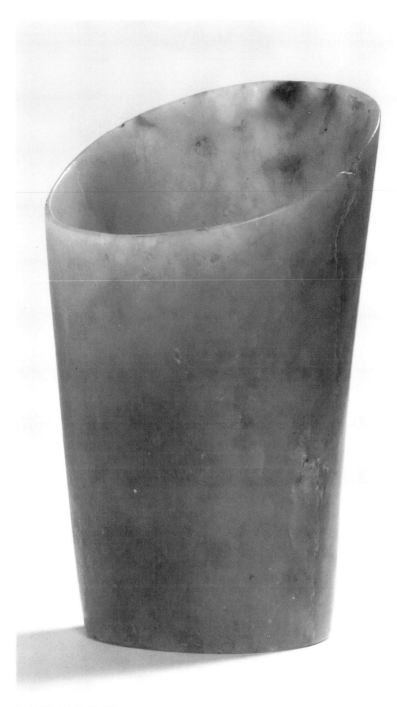

1. JADE HAIR CUFF
Neolithic, Hongshan culture, ca. 3500–2000 B.C., H. 15.2 cm (B60 J226)

had jade pendants in the form of turtles, birds, and dragons. We can only speculate on the precise symbolism of these neolithic burial jades, but their sheer number makes it clear that by the third millennium B.C. an association between jade jewels and life after death was already clearly established.

This association was perpetuated in the Shang dynasty (sixteenth–eleventh century B.C.), when the incidence of jades and other precious stones in burial proliferated. Much of the symbolism of the Liangzhu culture reappeared, sometimes in different media such as bronze, suggesting a continuation of Liangzhu concepts. Anyang Tomb no. 5, the final resting place of Fu Hao, probably the wife of King Wu Ding of the Shang dynasty and a woman of tremendous influence in her day (ca. 1300 B.C.), has provided the richest single cache of Shang dynasty jade jewels ever found—plaques, laminae, and small sculptures in the round. The more than 750 pieces excavated, excluding small flat discs and fragments, constitute a veritable summary of Shang jade production. There are pendants in the shape of tigers, tortoises, birds, rabbits, deer, humans, the ubiquitous fish (arched or not), praying mantises, and a single cicada; ridged, flanged, plain, and sectioned discs; thick archer's rings (e.g., no. 2), hairpins, and bracelets; as well as *cong* tubes of Liangzhu design, perhaps imports or heirlooms. Many flat pieces were pierced, either to be worn as pendants or to be sewn onto garments as laminae.

In all, Fu Hao's tomb contained more than enough jade to cover her entire body. If nothing else, the sheer volume testifies to the regard she enjoyed in life; her assignment of a posthumous name demonstrates that she continued to be an object of reverence and sacrifice even after death. Although the Shang did not leave much clear evidence of their beliefs about jade, jewelry, or the quality of life after death, by the Zhou dynasty (eleventh–third century B.C.), burial practices and burial raiment were much more rigidly systematized. The posthumous life had taken on a more worldly form, and by the end of the dynasty at least, the pursuit of physical immortality came to occupy some of the best scientific minds of the period.

Fueling this search was the idea, made explicit in the late Zhou, that certain substances, particularly jade, could prevent the corruption of the corpse and bring about physical immortality. One fourth-century B.C. Taoist adept, Chisongzi, actually ate ground jade suspended in blood, hoping to slough off his body and become a "corpse-free immortal" (*shijie xian*), and the kings of Zhou regularly ate jade as an act of ritual purification and abstention. Even more typical was the practice of plugging the orifices of the body with jade and other precious substances, the rationale for which was described much later by the fourth-century scholar Ge Hong:

2. SET OF SIX JADE ARCHER'S RINGS WITH A WOODEN CASE
Qing, Qianlong period, 1736–95, H. (case) 11.4 cm (B62 M51)

When jade and gold are inserted into the nine orifices, corpses do
not decay. When salt and brine are absorbed into the flesh and
marrow, dried meats do not spoil. So when men ingest substances
which are able to benefit their bodies and lengthen their days,
why should it be strange that (some of these) should confer life
perpetual?[1]

By the end of the Zhou, the collection of nine orifice plugs was
amplified into veils composed of many intricately carved pieces of jade
that shrouded the face and chest. Many of the small pendants and
laminae dating to the Spring and Autumn and Warring States periods
(eighth–third century B.C.) now in modern jade collections may once
have fitted into these elegant veils, and small, three-dimensional pieces,
either tongue-shaped cicadas (symbols of rejuvenation and rebirth)
or simple cylindrical plugs, were probably part of sets of orifice plugs.
    The presentation of these mortuary jewels was a great, even
princely privilege. *Liji* (Ritual Record, compiled in the early Han)
describes the reverence with which the prince's messenger delivered a
mouth jade to the son of the deceased; some of these must have been
used in burial, but a man with many admirers might receive several.
Even families whose means were limited tried to provide their dead

3. SIX JADE CICADAS, ANCIENT AND ARCHAISTIC
Top, left to right: Han, 206 B.C.–A.D. 220 (or later), H. 6.3 cm (B60 J594); Late Song, 10th–
13th c., H. 5.7 cm (B60 J543); Ming, 14th–17th c. (or later), H. 4.2 cm (B60 J727). Bottom,
left to right: Western Zhou, 10th–8th c. B.C., H. 3.9 cm (B60 J710); Late Zhou–Western Han,
5th–1st c. B.C., H. 2.8 cm (B60 J574); Song, 11th–13th c., H. 5.7 cm (B60 J584)

with cicada-shaped mouth amulets (no. 3), preferably of jade, but also,
in the Han dynasty, of less costly glass.

By the Western Han (206 B.C.–A.D. 9), the wealthiest dead were
completely encased in fitted suits of articulated jade, joined with wires
of gold, silver, or copper, depending on rank. The suit of Emperor
Wudi (r. 140–86 B.C.), described in *Xijing zaji* (Miscellaneous Records
of the Western Capital) as carved with dragons, phoenixes, tortoises,
and unicorns, was thought to be a flight of the writer's fancy until the
discovery in 1968 at Mancheng, Hebei, of two complete jade burial
suits dating to the late second century B.C., one made for Liu Sheng,
prince of Zhongshan, the other for his wife, Dou Wan. Liu Sheng's
suit, complete with articulated fingers, consisted of 2,500 pieces of
jade, tied together with gold wire to indicate that he was a prince of
imperial blood; Dou Wan, substantially smaller, was outfitted with

4. SIX BELT HOOKS
Left to right: Warring States, ca. 3rd c. B.C., L. 13.6–21 cm (B66 B8, B65 B43, B65 B27, B66 B5); Han, 206 B.C.–A.D. 220, L. 22.8 cm (B66 B4); Western Han, 2nd–1st c. B.C., L. 14.6 cm (B66 B3)

2,160 pieces. Since 1968 other jade suits have been excavated, including a second-century example made for Liu Gong, prince of Pengcheng (present-day Shandong). The custom, though costly, was considered beneficial well into the last years of the Han, so much so that some of the less wealthy dead were attired in ersatz suits of glass.

By the late Zhou and Han dynasties the Chinese had created a whole array of jewels aimed at preserving the body so that the dead might really enjoy immortality. Other life-sustaining requirements were also fulfilled. Along with detailed ceramic models of houses, granaries, pigpens, watchtowers, guardian dogs and warriors, entertainers, and servants, the Han carefully supplied their dead with crockery, sacrificial vessels, mirrors, clothing, and all the refined ornaments they had worn in life. We have to assume, based on the evidence of contemporary Han wall paintings, stone engravings, and tomb sculpture, that the elegant inlaid bronze belt hooks (no. 4), hairpins, bracelets, and girdle ornaments (no. 5) found in late Zhou and Han tombs were used by the living and that their placement in tombs was an attempt to replicate the world of the deceased for his or her pleasure after death.

JEWELS FOR THE LIVING
The Zhou dynasty *Odes*, compiled from the ninth century B.C. on, portray a bejeweled world. Horse bits were hung with bells and helmets embossed with shells; ladies and gentlemen wore ear ornaments dangling from silken threads, and gently tinkling ornaments of jade hung

5. FOUR JADE ORNAMENTS

Top to bottom: Western Zhou–Spring and Autumn period, 10th–6th c. B.C., L. 13.3 cm
(B60 J811); Early Warring States, ca. 5th c. B.C., L. 8.9 cm (B60 J528); Warring States,
ca. 3rd c. B.C., L. 15.5 cm (B60 J663); Western Han, 206 B.C.–A.D. 9, L. 9.5 cm (B60 J679)

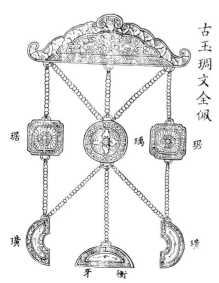

6. Drawing of an ancient jade pendant girdle,
from Berthold Laufer, *Jade: A Study in Chinese
Archaeology and Religion* (South Pasadena,
Calif.: P. D. and Ione Perkins, 1946).

from their belts. Their hair, sometimes false, was held in place with ivory combs, and their friendships were sealed with jade belt ornaments. Jewelry was an object of social exchange, given so that "friendship might be lasting,"[2] but also, as we have seen above, as a noble act of reverence to the dead.

By the last centuries of the Zhou, the jewels that could or could not be worn by different ranks of people were distinctly outlined. The main symbolic gem, or group of gems (in a sense analogous to the jade veil worn by the dead), was the elaborate *pei*, or girdle ornament (no. 6). Hung in rigid order from the belt, its pieces softly sounded as the wearer moved but were silenced, as a sign of respect, in the presence of royalty or in one's father's room. The elements of the *pei*, each with its own name, were carved in abstract shapes—round, arched, square, triangular, and as two half-discs, which, when joined, formed a miniature *bi* disc. Each piece was also carved overall with powerful natural images—scrolling tigers and dragons or curled rice sprouts.

Gems, especially jade, not only represented the finest moral and social virtues, "pure trust" and reciprocity, but could actually impart them to the wearer. So strongly were the *pei* associated with the proprieties described in the *Odes* that even the third-century poet Cao Zhi cast a romantic exchange of jewels in classic terms, evoking images of gentility and social finesse. The poet offers a girdle jade to his lady as an affectionate pledge and, totally smitten, wrote:

> Ah, the pure trust of the lovely lady,
> Trained in ritual, acquainted with the Odes;
> She holds up a garnet stone to match my gift.[3]

Because jewelry in early China was so intimately connected with conspicuous displays of wealth and status, just as is it today, its elaboration and ultimately the confusion of its meaning could not be controlled, try as conservative Confucians might. By the late Zhou and Han, the girdle ornaments of jade and other precious stones that are so purely conceived in the classic ritual texts attributed to the Zhou were, like burial jades, a source of inspiration and fancy. Gorgeous plaques in animal shapes (especially tigers, dragons, and birds), belt hooks in jade or gilt metal inlaid with silver and turquoise, and buckles conceived as intertwined animals, mostly worn by gentlemen, continued to focus on the waist, but with much greater creative latitude. In the Tang dynasty (618–906), the leather or silk belt, simply linked together with a belt hook, gave way to a new fashion, a wider leather belt, possibly of Central Asian origin, embossed with metal repoussé plaques decorated with exotic animals (no. 7). This fashion was developed even further in the Ming (1368–1644), when emperors went to their graves wearing heavy belts composed of intricately carved jade plaques. All these fashions

7. GILT COPPER BELT PLAQUES WITH DEER(?)
Tang dynasty, 618–906, H. 4 cm (B68 B10a–g)

had great longevity; the belt hooks of the late Zhou and Han, for example, were revived periodically (but most notably in the Song, 960–1279, and Qing, 1644–1911), when a taste for the archaic and antique reigned.

Fascination with rare, foreign materials caught the Chinese fancy very early, but at no time with greater force than in the Tang, when China was in close touch with vast regions in Central and Southeast Asia. These distant, often wild lands and their limitless bounty generated new fashions among ladies and gentlemen both (high boots, face painting, and skirts covered with feathers are but a few) and inspired the lush, brilliant poetry of Tang writers, who described wonders as diverse as diadems of living fireflies and frangipani blossoms, worn by princesses of the coral atolls, and river sprites with bird-shaped headdresses, whose torsos were covered with pearls.[4]

Such images were a constant stimulus to the creativity of jewelers and their cosmopolitan Tang clients, whose personal adornments were made of materials carried to the capital at Chang'an from the frontiers of the empire. Jade and lapis came from the deserts of Central Asia, pearls from the South Seas, hornbill and feathers from the highland mountains of the south. A favorite was the iridescent blue feather of the kingfisher, a bird that thrives even around the ponds of northern China but is found in greatest numbers in the southern mountains, where, the poet Zhou Yao wrote, "elephants trample sagwire leaves and . . . men gather halcyon plumage."[5] The delicate feathers were fitted into armatures of gilt wire and embellished with *granulé* gold to make butterfly- and bird-shaped hair ornaments that trembled with every movement and captured the imagination of Chinese ladies and their admirers well into the twentieth century; probably the most glorious example is the early seventeenth-century ruby-, pearl-, and sapphire-studded crown of Xiaoduan, consort of the Ming dynasty Emperor

8. FOUR BELT HOOKS AND BUCKLES, ANCIENT AND ARCHAISTIC
Left to right: Jade half-buckle, Warring States, 5th–3rd c. B.C., L. 6.4 cm (B60 J453); hornbill buckle, Qing, 18th–19th c., L. 10.4 cm (B65 J14); coral belt hook, Qing, 18th c., L. 9.5 cm (B60 J578); jade buckle, Qing, 18th c., L. 11.6 cm (B86 J10)

Wanli (r. 1573–1620), a spherical fantasy of dragons, phoenixes, and clouds. These elegant and courtly ornaments were made primarily for visual, not moral, effect; their exoticism is stimulating and alluring by design, even if ultimately tamed and civilized. Omitted from Tang and later descriptions of aigrettes, gold-stemmed hairpins, and head ornaments of halcyon feathers is the moral message carried by so many jewels of the Zhou and Han.

Many jewels and ornaments of later dynasties replay forms developed much earlier. Some consciously copy archaic forms; others are outright forgeries, made to deceive. Still others create more subtle links with the past, injecting ancient shapes with new meaning. Belt hooks and buckles were often designed, in the Ming and Qing dynasties, to look exactly like Han pieces, but others use the same basic design and add new decorative elements—flowers, plants, and other motifs— combined into meaningful rebuses, or visual puns (no. 8).[6] This type of auspicious design dominated the decorative arts from the late Ming onward, so that a well-dressed person, from embroidered shoes to belt to hat, could be a veritable signboard of wishes for good fortune, long life, success, and fertility.

The refinements of dress for the upper classes called for all sorts of ornaments for the head, including those that clearly indicated rank, such as jade topknots (no. 9) and official caps with finials of precious gems, and other purely decorative items, such as earrings, hairpins, and headdresses. For the waist there were buckles, pouches, tinderboxes, flints, cases for mirrors and fans, and dangling ornaments of embroidered silk or jade, and for the wrists, fingers, and nails there were

9. JADE HAT-SHAPED TOPKNOT COVER
Ming dynasty, 1368–1644, H. 4.4 cm (B60 J608)

10. FOUR HAIR ORNAMENTS
Qing dynasty, 18th c., gilt silver and kingfisher feathers, H. 16.5 cm (pin)
(B62 M45)

bangles, rings, and talon-like nail covers of worked metal or jade worn by people of perfect leisure.

By the last years of the Qing dynasty, the process of dressing a lady's hair alone could take more than two hours. The hair was first brushed, pomaded, pinned up on a framework, augmented if necessary with false hair, and only then decorated with ornaments in jade, gold, coral, pearls, silk, and kingfisher feathers, in the shape of flowers, butterflies, birds, and fantastic fairy dwellings (no. 10). Many of these jewels were totally artificial creations, but others actually incorporated real blooms.

In the Qing dynasty Chinese dress was also complicated by the fact that the ruling dynasty was not ethnically Han, but Manchu. The Manchu rulers used their robes, with tight, "horse-hoof" cuffs, and their court hats, beads, and rank badges to set themselves and their subjects apart from earlier, native Chinese dynasties. Even though they rapidly lost all but the most superficial ability to speak their own language, well into the waning years of the dynasty they still maintained their own ways of dress, refusing, for example, to allow their women's feet to be bound (they wore shoes set up on tiny pedestals instead). Manchu ladies also wore large black horned headdresses that were derived from the way Mongol women dressed and encased their long hair into two ram-like horns. But the Manchu were sufficiently sinicized that their headdresses, though traditional in shape, were covered with pearls, dangling jades, and kingfisher ornaments set on springs, ideas taken from their Han Chinese sisters. In the last years of the Chinese empire, everyone, Manchu and Han alike, vacillated in dress between a rigid traditionalism and a robust, curious eclecticism. The result was that their jewelry, made of the rarest and most exotic materials they could afford, created a deeply engaging fantasy where all the senses—sight, sound, and even scent, could be aroused.

Patricia Berger
Curator of Chinese Art

NOTES

1. See Joseph Needham, *Science and Civilization in China*, vol. V.2 (Cambridge: Cambridge University Press, 1974), pp. 284ff.

2. James Legge, trans., *The Chinese Classics*, 2d ed., vol. 4, *The She-king* (Hong Kong: Hong Kong University Press, 1960), pp. 107–108.

3. Burton Watson, ed. and trans., *The Columbia Book of Chinese Poetry* (New York: Columbia University Press, 1984), p. 119.

4. Edward H. Schafer, *The Vermilion Bird* (Berkeley and Los Angeles: University of California Press, 1967), p. 86; and *The Divine Woman* (Berkeley, Los Angeles, and London: University of California Press, 1973), pp. 54, 113, and infra.

5. Schafer, *The Vermilion Bird*, p. 238.

6. See Terese Tse Bartholomew, *Myths and Rebuses in Chinese Art* (San Francisco: Asian Art Museum, 1988).

KOREA

Recent excavations reveal that Koreans during the Three Kingdoms period (57 B.C.–A.D. 668) adorned themselves resplendently with crowns, girdles, caps, earrings, bracelets, necklaces, and rings, made primarily of gold but also of silver, bronze, jade crystals, and glass.[1] The most spectacular symbols of power and authority from ancient Korea are undoubtedly the gold crowns that have been discovered in all three kingdoms—Koguryŏ, Paekche, and Silla. Those discovered in several undisturbed tombs of the Silla kingdom in Kyŏngju have especially astonished the world with their flamboyant form and dazzling array of small spangles, pendants, and comma-shaped jade or gold pieces. The crowns are made of thin sheet gold cut into a headband that supports several upright pieces. The uprights represent the abstracted forms of branched trees and deer antlers important in shamanism. The surface of Silla crowns are decorated with tiny punched dots arranged in horizontal and vertical rows as well as in scallop or sawtooth designs. Numerous small circular or heart-shaped spangles and comma-shaped jade pieces are attached by means of twisted gold wire, enhancing the shimmering effect. The most luxurious gold crown, with three pairs of pendants and a bursting array of comma-shaped jades and gold spangles (no. 1), was discovered in a lady's tomb in the north mound of the Great Tomb at Hwangnam, Kyŏngju,[2] suggesting that Silla gold crowns were worn by both men and women of the ruling class.

Related to the gold crowns are simpler diadems, caps, and cap ornaments from the Three Kingdoms period decorated with openwork floral, flame, or geometric designs. The most unusual diadem is one in the form of the outstretched wings of a bird from the Heavenly Horse Tomb, Kyŏngju.[3] Gold, silver, and bronze were the most popularly used metals for the crowns as well as for small diadems, caps, and cap ornaments.

Next to Silla gold crowns, gold girdles from Kyŏngju tombs are most impressive to behold. Girdles, undoubtedly important personal ornaments, were made by horizontally connecting square openwork plaques. Each plaque supports a buckle-shaped loop. Below the loops are a dozen or more long pendants consisting of alternating square and oblong plaques. At the end of each pendant is attached an ingenious ornament such as a fish, incense container, needle, tweezers, sheathed

1. Gold ornamentation from an excavation site at the north mound of the Great Tomb at Hwangnam, Kyŏngju. Three Kingdoms period, Silla, 5th–6th c.

knife, tassel, rectangular tablet, or comma-shaped jewel. All the pendants are about equal in length and size except for one, which is longer and larger. This major pendant is placed off center, usually over the left or right leg of the deceased.

The Asian Art Museum's pendant (1991.220), fish in openwork (1991.221), and comma-shaped jewel (1991.215) must have once been part of a silver girdle (no. 2). The pendant is made of alternating large and small oblong forms cut from sheet silver; at the end is a rectangular tablet embellished with rolled edges and connected by a plaque reinforced with four rivets.

Numerous beautiful earrings have been unearthed from Three Kingdoms tombs. Among the most luxurious are those discovered from the tombs of Paekche King Muryong in Kongju and the Heavenly Horse Tomb in Kyŏngju. Despite decorative differences, the earrings share three distinctive parts: a main ring at the top, a middle section connected to the main ring that supports the last and third section, which is in the form of one or more short pendants. Earrings are usually divided into two groups: those with a thin main ring, which can be hollow or solid, and those with a thick, hollow main ring.

The surfaces of the gold earrings are often delicately ornamented with hexagonal, circular, diamond, or floral designs in granulation and inset with small colored glass or stone. The dangling sections are ingeniously assembled with clusters of flat or curved leaves or heart-shaped spangles and tiny hollow spheres; comma-shaped jade pieces,

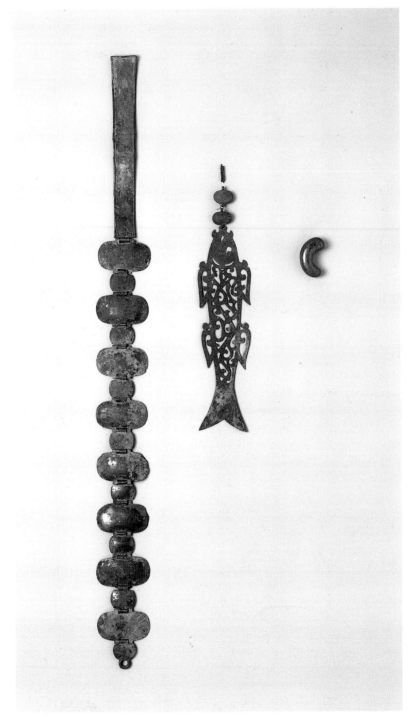

2. SILVER PENDANT, FISH, AND JEWEL
Three Kingdoms period, Silla, 5th–6th c. Pendant: L. 70.5 cm (1991.220); fish: L. 28 cm
(1991.221); jewel: L. 4.4 cm (1991.215), collection of the Asian Art Museum of San Francisco

3. GOLD EARRINGS
Left to right: Three Kingdoms period, Silla, 5th–6th c., L. 5.7 cm, collection of the Asian Art
Museum of San Francisco (1991.214.1–.2); Three Kingdoms period, Kaya, 5th–6th c., L. 8.7 cm
(anonymous loan); Three Kingdoms period, Silla, 5th–6th c., L. 6.5 cm, gift of Committee for
Korean Art (1991.227)

sometimes with gold caps decorated in granulation and inset with
gemstones, are also found.

A pair of gold earrings in the Asian Art Museum (no. 3, left) has a
thin, solid main ring supporting two unusual clusters of floral decora-
tions embellished in granulation. They in turn support a heart-shaped
form and two small spangles, one heart-shaped, the other circular.

For necklaces and bracelets, gold, silver, jade, amber, crystal, and
glass were used. Glass was certainly a popular material, for thousands
of glass beads have been unearthed from tombs of the Three Kingdoms
period. The most spectacular finds were made in the recently discovered
tomb of King Muryong at Kongju as well as in the Great Tomb at
Hwangnam, Kyŏngju.[4] Glass beads in dazzling colors—blue, green,
yellow, orange, red, and pink—were often assembled with narrow rectangular gold braces, comma-shaped jade pieces, and tiny gold balls
with or without leaf- or heart-shaped spangles (no. 4).

During the Unified Silla (668–935) and Koryŏ (918–1392) dynasties, personal ornaments continued to flourish. Written sources show
that the court was concerned about individuals who indulged themselves in luxurious personal adornments inappropriate to their status.[5]
Apparently Koreans at the time loved to wear richly embroidered silk
pouches with tassels and other ornaments made of ingenious macrame
designs, as can often be seen in Buddhist paintings of the Koryŏ dynasty.
Both men and women wore earrings until the latter part of the sixteenth century in the Chosŏn dynasty (1392–1910), since the earrings

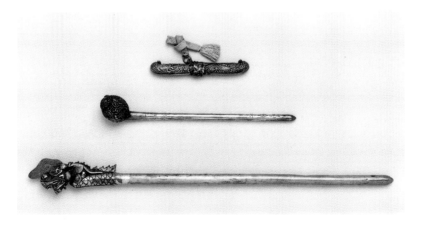

4. BEADS FOR NECKLACES

Three Kingdoms period, Silla, 5th–6th c. Left to right: silver, D. 9.5 cm (1991.216.1); gold,
D. 7.5 cm (1991.216.2); gold, L. 13 cm (1991.217); gold, L. 9.5 cm (1991.218), collection of the
Asian Art Museum of San Francisco

5. KNIFE AND HAIR ORNAMENTS

Chosŏn dynasty, 19th c. Top to bottom: ornamental knife (*changdo*), silver, L. 11.5 cm,
gift of Committee for Korean Art (1991.206); hairpin (*pinyŏ*), silver, L. 22.5 cm, gift of
Mrs. Chung-Hee Kim (1991.204); hairpin (*yongjam*), silver and gilt copper, L. 42.5 cm,
gift of Mrs. Chung-Hee Kim (1991.205)

6. PENDANTS WITH *NORIGAE*
Chosŏn dynasty, 19th c. Left to right: three-gourd *norigae*, silver, enamel colors, silk, L. 25 cm, gift of the Matsubara Memorial Fund (1991.201); incense-box *norigae*, brass, silk, L. 27 cm, gift of Francesca M. Bacon, Committee for Korean Art, and the Matsubara Memorial Fund (1991.202); three-pepper *norigae*, silver, enamel colors, silk, L. 27.5 cm, gift of Mrs. Suno Osterweis (1991.203)

of those born of gentry were exempt from a 1429 edict prohibiting the wasteful use of gold and silver.[6] But in 1572 pierced ears were finally prohibited by law. After this, earrings were made with a large cumbersome loop to be worn over the ear and used only on special occasions such as weddings.

Rings, *pinyŏ* (hair bars), and other hair ornaments (no. 5) continued to occupy a special place in the hearts of women. The ideal was to wear rings and *pinyŏ* of gold in winter and jade in summer. During the eighteenth and nineteenth centuries *norigae* (playful objects) captivated the attention of Korean women of all classes (no. 6). These small silver ornaments accented with enamel colors came in the forms of

7. In this painting by Shin Yun-bok (Korean, 18th c.), a woman attaches
an ornamental tassel to the ribbon that fastens her blouse. Kansong Museum
of Fine Art, Seoul.

gourds, peppers, butterflies, fish, cicadas, bats, turtles, ducks, knives,
and coin pouches. They were attached to silk macrame with long tassels and worn over women's blouses or belts, as can be seen in paintings
by Kim Hong-do (1745–before 1818) and Shin Yun-bok (fl. late eighteenth century, no. 7). *Norigae*, often worn in threes, not only en-
hanced the beauty of *hanbok*, Korean dress, but also reflected the
wearer's wishes for a happy marriage, many sons, health, wealth, and
long life. Each playful object contained auspicious symbolism: for
example, peppers for many sons, ducks for happy marriage, and fish for
abundance (1991.201–206).

Kumja Paik Kim
Curator of Korean Art

NOTES

1. Han Byong-sam, ed., *Kobun misul* (Old tomb art), Han'guk ui Mi 22 (Seoul: Chung'ang
Ilbosa, 1985), pp. 1–191.

2. *Special Exhibition of Relics from the Tomb No. 98, Kyongju*, exh. cat. (Seoul: National Museum
of Korea, 1975), pls. 1, 22; Han Byong-sam, ed., *Kobun misul*, pls. 1–2, p. 202.

3. Han Byong-sam, ed., *Kobun misul*, pl. 44.

4. Ibid., pls. 16–17, 19–21, 153–54, 156.

5. Sok Chu-son, "Han'guk Pokshik ui Pyongchon" (History of Korean costumes), in *Han'guk ui
Mi*, exh. cat. (Seoul, National Museum of Korea, 1988), pp. 132–72.

6. Chang Suk-hwan, "Choson shidae ui momchirye" (Personal ornaments during the Choson
dynasty), in *Han'guk ui Mi*, pp. 34–35.

JAPAN

Personal use of ornamental objects is found in very early prehistoric and early historic times in Japan, and again in a relatively late period, beginning in the mid-sixteenth century. During the interim, only on formal court occasions did women adorn their hair with ornaments, which were based on older designs. The styles and materials of the early period must have been similar to those of islands to the south and continental Asian neighbors.[1] Necklaces and bracelets of the prehistoric periods were simply made of beautiful seashells, animal tusks, and other natural, semiprecious materials. Later, ornaments were fabricated of manufactured materials such as colorful glass beads and precious metals. Many refined pieces were actually imported from the continent along with their accompanying technologies and craftsmen, who probably made similar objects in Japan and, at the same time, trained native artisans.

Two *haniwa* figures are good examples of early fashions (no. 1). Possibly female shamans, the figures wear necklaces most likely made of comma-shaped beads and circular hair ornaments. Both men and women undoubtedly used combs for practical purposes, but judging from existing *haniwa*, only women wore them as decoration (no. 2). Combs were made most commonly of wood or bamboo. Lacquer was sometimes added for its strength and decorative qualities. The fragmented remains of such combs have been excavated from Jōmon sites dating to several thousand years B.C.

During the Heian period (794–1185), famous for the intense Japanization of all aspects of life, fashion changed completely. Garments for men and women became voluminous, with the main aesthetic interest focused on color. In particular, women's fashion emphasized carefully chosen colors arranged in multiple layers of silk. Special names alluding to flowers and seasonal interests were assigned to various combinations.

To balance the heavy volume of the new garments, women's coiffures changed from the Chinese-type topknot to a loose, naturally flowing style. The thickness and the length of shiny, straight black hair was the center of a woman's beauty. As well documented by Lady Sei Shōnagon (fl. late tenth century), the new style was praised by both female and male admirers.[2] Hairpieces were used by less fortunate

1. FEMALE *HANIWA* WITH NECKLACES AND FACE PAINTING
Late Kofun period, 6th c., earthenware, H. 60 and 61 cm (B60 S164+, S165+)

2. FEMALE *HANIWA* WEARING A COMB
Late Kofun period, 6th c., earthenware, H. 17.1 cm (B62 P6+)

women with poor natural hair, and long hair became a precious commodity within a ready market. To contrast their dark hair, women used white face powder accented with a touch of lip rouge. To emphasize the fair skin of the face, they applied blackening to the teeth. Powdering the face and blackening the teeth were also practiced by court nobles, who wore body incense as well.

In the Kamakura (1185–1333) and Muromachi (1392–1573) periods a less stable political and social climate freed men and women of the upper class from their confining garments and hairstyles. Tooth blackening and the use of facial cosmetics, however, continued among court nobles, whose practices were even imitated by some of the fashionable samurai population. Women began wearing their hair shorter and tying it back simply, but it was the generally playful social trends of the Momoyama period (1573–1615) that changed many styles of adornment. Women performers who dressed as young men in early Momoyama Kabuki theater performances wore their hair tied in the hairstyle of young men. Other female entertainers quickly followed this trend in an even bolder manner that eventually came to change the hairdos of the female population.

Historically, the Japanese male, with his more active life, simply tied up his hair, sometimes to secure official headgear or to more easily don battle helmets. Men's hairdos did not change much with time; women's, however, developed into some of the most sophisticated and complex hairstyles in the world. It was this passion for various coiffures that prompted the emergence of new types of hair ornaments. Combs, known since earliest times in both functional and ornamental modes, showed a remarkable development as purely decorative accessories (no. 3). Hairpins (*kanzashi*), which had disappeared at about the same time Chinese-style topknots did, eventually had a strong revival. The straight, ornamental hair stick (*kōgai*) was devised to help secure certain types of hairdos and eventually became more decorative than functional (no. 5).

Craftsmen spared no effort in designing and executing fine hair ornaments. Lacquered wooden combs and hair sticks were decorated with gold and silver *makie* (sprinkled designs) and sometimes inlaid with mother-of-pearl, coral, and other semiprecious materials. Tortoiseshell ornaments made of imported shells were much treasured. While shell ornaments were decorated like those made of lacquered wood, the most treasured pieces were left undecorated to show the fine markings of the natural shell (no. 4, top). A high-quality example of such a comb in the Genroku era (1688–1703) would have cost as much as two *ryō*, or two pieces of gold,[3] a sum large enough to purchase rice to feed a small family for months.

The leg bone of a crane, in its concise size and suitable shape, was a choice found object from which to make lacquered and gold-decorated

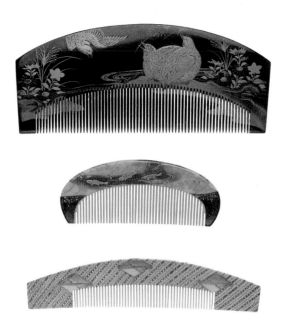

3. COMBS
Late Edo period, 19th c., lacquerwork. Top to bottom: quails and autumn plants,
L. 12.5 cm; fish in stream, L. 7.9 cm; double fan, L. 11.6 cm, gifts of Harry and
Edith Marks (1989.40.15,.9,.7)

kōgai (no. 5, middle and lower middle). More important, the bird was
a symbol of longevity, and its bone must have been prized. Glass, a
newly popularized material, was also made into combs and other ornaments for fun-loving and fashionable women. It was either used alone
as *kōgai* (no. 5, bottom) and *kanzashi* (no. 5, top) or combined with
a more traditional material to create a transparent section in an
ornament.

These preferences appeared in the Edo period (1615–1868) as a
highly structured class system was also emerging. Unwritten laws
restricted women from wearing hairdos not proper for their social or
marital status; written law prohibited women from spending large sums
on hair ornaments. Until about the 1650s certain types, such as genu-
ine tortoiseshell combs, were singled out as ornaments only the wives
of *daimyō* (provincial lords) were allowed to wear. During the late Edo
and into the Meiji period (1868–1912) a matching set of comb and
kōgai became fashionable for married women to arrange in a standard
hairdo called *marumage* (no. 6).

Tooth blackening continued to be an important part of personal
adornment for married women. An elaborate set of personal tooth-
blackening implements made of lacquered wood (no. 7) was included in
any large trousseau. The custom was abolished as unhygienic during

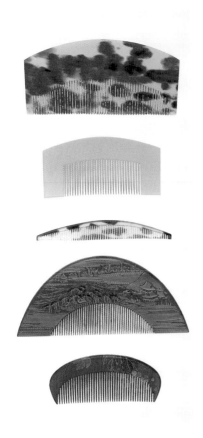

4. COMBS
Mid to late Edo period, 18th–19th c. Top
to bottom: tortoiseshell with markings,
L. 11.6 cm; plain tortoiseshell, L. 8.8 cm;
tortoiseshell with markings, L. 10.1 cm; land-
scape in gold, silver, and lacquer on wood,
L. 12.7 cm; grapes on vine in gold and silver
lacquer on wood, L. 8.4 cm (anonymous loans)

the Meiji period when Western influence spread throughout Japan,
although modern science has proved that the practice had some merit
in preventing tooth decay.

For the samurai, who had little chance to sport their arms and
armor during the generally peaceful Edo period, the focus of personal
adornment was the carved netsuke and small, compartmented medi-
cine cases called *inrō*. Affluent merchants joined the samurai by
wearing netsuke from which they suspended tobacco pouches and pipe
cases. These small items were meant to exhibit personal taste through
adornment, just as modern fashion-conscious people purchase designer
jewelry. A new design or an interesting idea by a truly creative crafts-
man would attract many eager customers as well as prompt imitators
producing less attractive merchandise for less discriminating tastes.

An *inrō* and netsuke were connected by a double cord with a slid-
ing bead (*ojime*, literally "cord binder") that tightened the cord and
held the tiered sections of the *inrō* together (see back cover). The
netsuke, fastened onto one end of the cord, was then slipped under
a man's narrow obi, allowing the *inrō* or other small articles to hang
freely at his side.

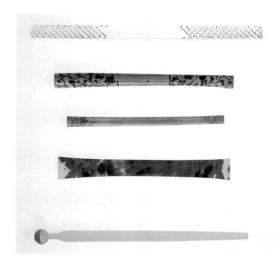

5. HAIRPINS

Mid to late Edo period, 18th–19th c. Top to bottom: clear cut glass,
L. 20.3 cm; plant scroll in gold lacquer on crane leg bone, L. 15.6 cm;
autumn plants in gold lacquer on crane leg bone, L. 13.7 cm; land-
scape in gold lacquer on tortoiseshell, L. 15 cm; amber-color glass,
L. 18.6 cm (anonymous loans)

6. This detail from a painting by Hosoda Eishi (1756–1829) depicts a hairdo reserved
for the highest-ranking courtesans of the Edo period (B60 D81). The woman wears a set
of three flat combs, twelve *kanzashi*, a long *kogai*, and a few shorter *kushi-dome* pins that
help to keep the large combs in place. The set appears to be of tortoiseshell, a highly
treasured material for such ornaments.

The *inrō* and netsuke of a set frequently shared a decorative theme
and were sometimes made of the same material. Some sets appear to
have been commissioned, occasionally reflecting a client's occupation
or, more frequently, representing the animal of the zodiac corresponding to the wearer's birth date. Judging from the numerous surviving

7. COSMETIC SET
Late Edo period, early 19th c., lacquerwork, H. (cabinet) 34.5 cm, gift of Mr. and
Mrs. George F. Jewett, Jr. (1991.133.1–.13)

examples of fine *inrō* and netsuke, men were just as vain and discriminating as women, but definitely more extravagant and acquisitive.
Women quite often treasured a single fine comb and hairpin, which
sometimes were given up in times of family need, contributing to the
dispersal and eventual destruction of many of these objects.

In Japan, unlike other Asian countries where precious metals and
fine gems were mostly treasured for their material value, personal
accessories did not enter the lives of women until very recent times.
Because the traditional kimono—still preferred for formal occasions—
does not take the complement of necklaces or earrings, conventional
personal ornaments tend to be viewed as simple accessories.

Yoshiko Kakudo
Curator of Japanese Art

NOTES

1. Inhabitants of the Ryūkyū Islands, for instance, exchanged their shell ornaments for pottery
from Kyushu; see Richard Pearson, "Chiefly Exchange between Kyushu and Okinawa, Japan, in
the Yayoi Period," *Antiquity* 64, no. 245 (Dec. 1990), p. 911.

2. *The Pillow Book of Sei Shōnagon*, ed. and trans. Ivan Morris (New York: Penguin Books, 1971),
pp. 71 and 201.

3. Sumiko Hashimoto, *Yuigami to Kamikazari*, Nihon no Bijutsu, no. 23 (Tokyo: Shibundo,
1968), p. 95.

SELECTED BIBLIOGRAPHY

Boyer, Martha. *Mongol Jewellery.* Copenhagen: Gyldendalske Boghandel, Nordisk Forlag, 1952.

Brunel, Francis. *Jewellery of India: Five Thousand Years of Tradition.* New Delhi: National Book Trust, 1972.

Dubin, Lois Sherr. *The History of Beads from 30,000 B.C. to the Present.* New York: Harry N. Abrams, 1987.

Huh Dong-hwa and Pak Young-sook. *Crafts of the Inner Court.* Seoul: The Museum of Korean Embroidery, 1987.

Jahss, Melvin, and Betty Jahss. *Inro and Other Miniature Forms of Japanese Lacquer Art.* Rutland, Vt.: Charles E. Tuttle Company, 1971.

Kinsey, Robert O. *Ojime: Magical Jewels of Japan.* New York: Harry N. Abrams, 1991.

Laufer, Berthold. *Jade: A Study in Chinese Archaeology and Religion.* South Pasadena, Calif.: P.D. and Ione Perkins in cooperation with The Westwood Press and W.M. Hawley, 1946.

Miksic, John N. *Old Javanese Gold.* Singapore: Ideation, 1990.

Moorey, Peter Roger Stuart. "The Art of Ancient Iran," in *Ancient Bronzes, Ceramics, and Seals.* Los Angeles: Los Angeles County Museum of Art, 1981.

——— . *Catalogue of the Ancient Persian Bronzes in the Ashmolean Museum.* Oxford: Oxford University Press, 1971.

Muscarella, Oscar White. *Bronze and Iron: Ancient Near Eastern Artifacts in The Metropolitan Museum of Art.* New York: Metropolitan Museum of Art, 1981.

National Museum of Korea, *Han'guk ui Mi* (Beauty of Korea). Seoul: National Museum of Korea, 1988. Exhibition catalogue in Korean with English summaries and captions.

Ornament, A Quarterly of Jewelry & Personal Adornment (formerly *The Bead Journal*), Los Angeles, California.

Rodgers, Susan. *Power and Gold: Jewelry from Indonesia, Malaysia, and the Philippines.* Geneva: Barbier-Müller Museum, 1985.

Stronge, Susan, Nima Smith, and J.C. Harle. *A Golden Treasury: Jewellery from the Indian Subcontinent.* London: Victoria and Albert Museum in association with Mapin Publishing Pvt. Ltd., 1988.

Ueda, Reikichi. *The Netsuke Handbook.* Adapted from the Japanese by Raymond Bushell. Rutland, Vt.: Charles E. Tuttle Company, 1968.

Villegas, Ramon N. *Kayamanan: The Philippine Jewelry Tradition.* Manila: Bangko Sentral ng Pilipinas, 1983.

White, Joyce C. *Ban Chiang: Discovery of a Lost Bronze Age.* Philadelphia: The University Museum, University of Pennsylvania, 1982.